BIG-NOTE PIANO

THE BIG-NOTE HYMN BOOK

ISBN 978-1-4234-5965-1

HAL•LEONARD®
CORPORATION
7777 W. BLUEMOUND RD. P.O. BOX 13819 MILWAUKEE, WI 53213

In Australia Contact:
Hal Leonard Australia Pty. Ltd.
4 Lentara Court
Cheltenham, Victoria, 3192 Australia
Email: ausadmin@halleonard.com.au

Visit Hal Leonard Online at
www.halleonard.com

ABIDE WITH ME

Words by HENRY F. LYTE
Music by WILLIAM H. MONK

Peacefully

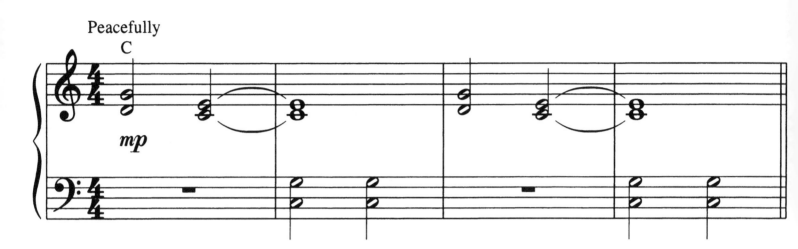

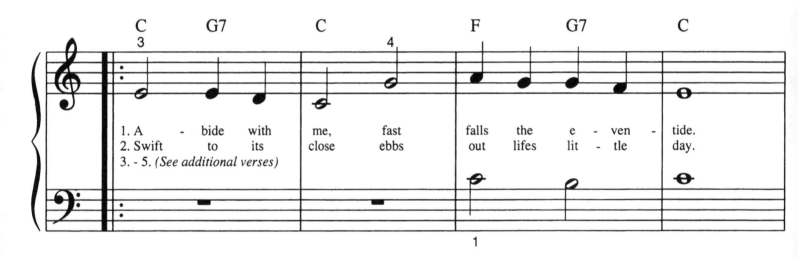

1. A - bide with me, fast falls the e - ven - tide.
2. Swift to its close fast ebbs out lifes lit - tle day.
3. - 5. *(See additional verses)*

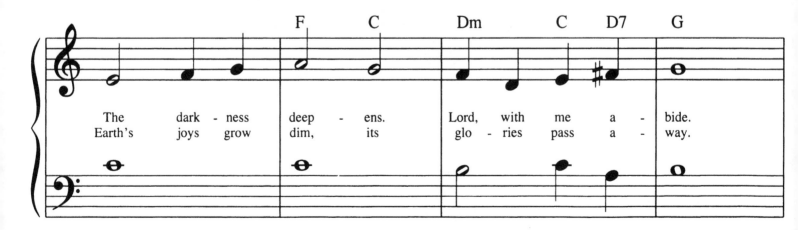

The dark - ness deep - ens. Lord, with me a - bide.
Earth's joys grow dim, its glo - ries pass a - way.

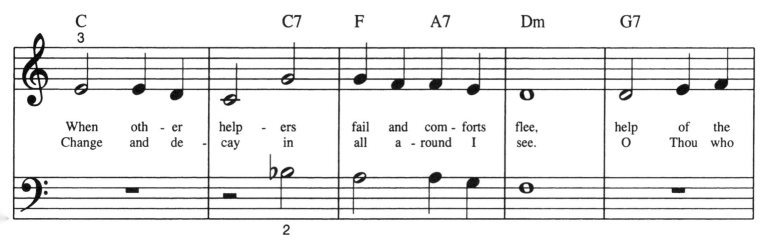

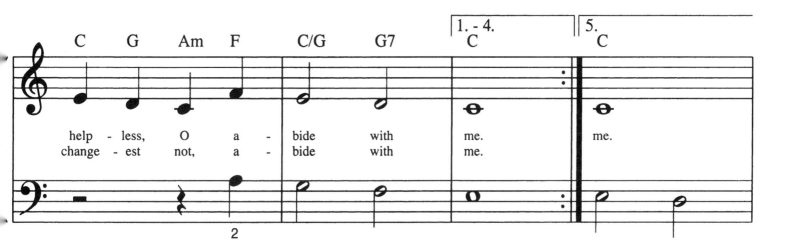

fading away like bells

Additional Verses

3. I need Thy presence every passing hour.
   What but Thy grace can foil the tempter's power?
   Who, like Thyself, my guide and stay can be?
   Through clouds and sunshine, Lord, abide with me.

4. I fear no foe, with Thee at hand to bless;
   ills have no weight, and tears no bitterness.
   Where is death's sting? Where, grave, thy victory?
   I triumph still, if thou abide with me.

5. Hold Thou Thy cross before my closing eyes;
   shine through the gloom and point me to the skies.
   Heaven's morning breaks, and earth's vain shadows flee;
   in life, in death, O Lord, abide with me.

AMAZING GRACE

Words by JOHN NEWTON
Traditional American Melody

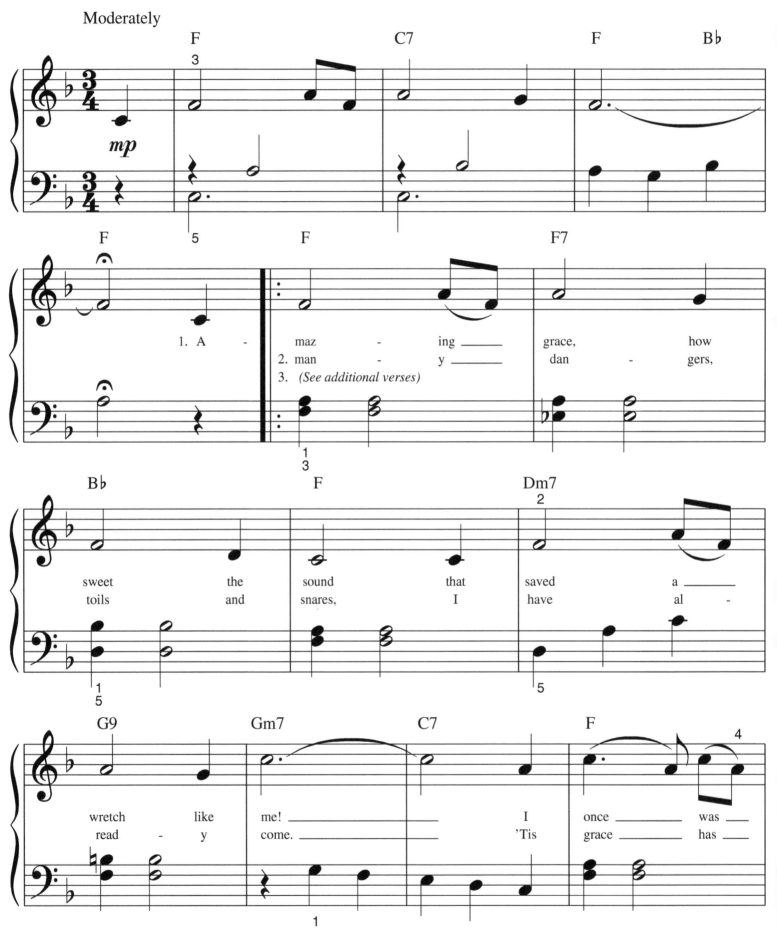

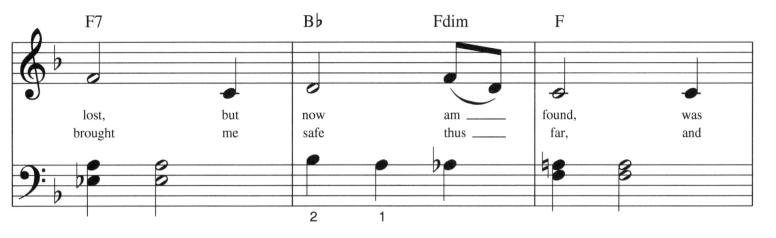

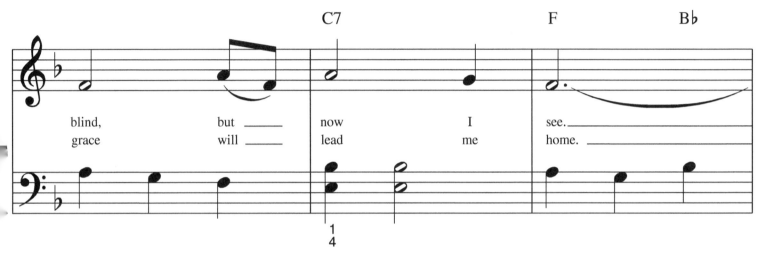

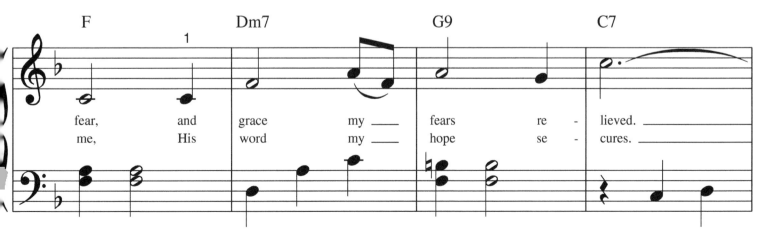

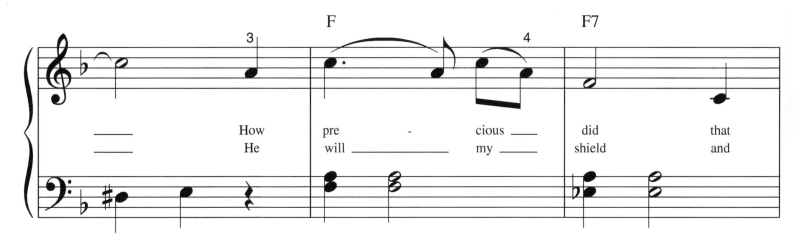

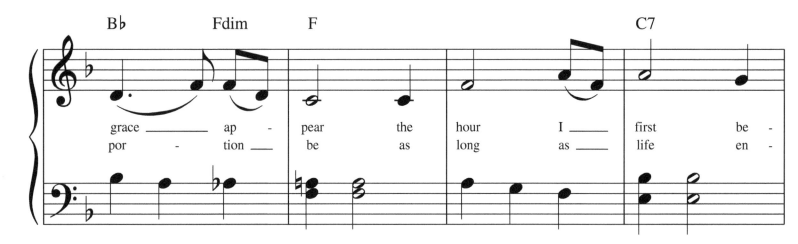

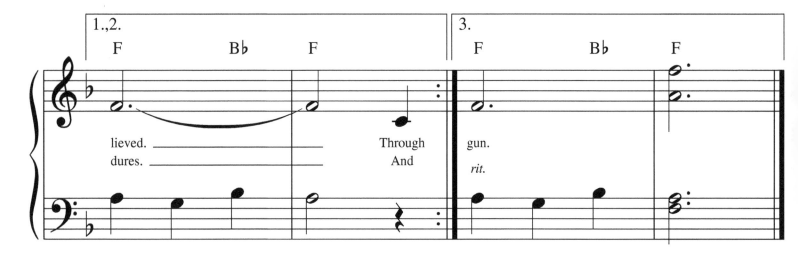

Additional Verses

3. And when this flesh and heart shall fail
   And mortal life shall cease.
   I shall possess within the veil
   A life of joy and peace.
   When we've been there ten thousand years,
   Bright shining as the sun,
   We've no less days to sing God's praise
   Than when we first begun.

ALL CREATURES OF OUR GOD AND KING

Words by FRANCIS OF ASSISI
Translated by WILLIAM HENRY DRAPER
Music from *Geistliche Kirchengesäng*

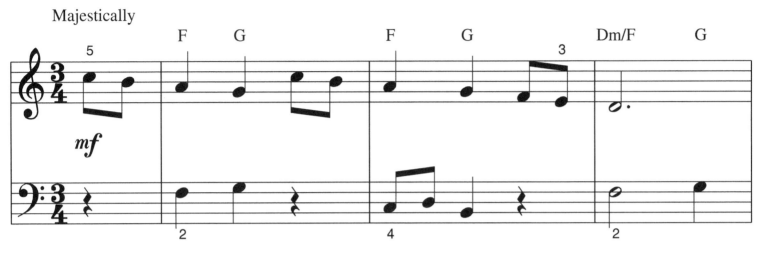

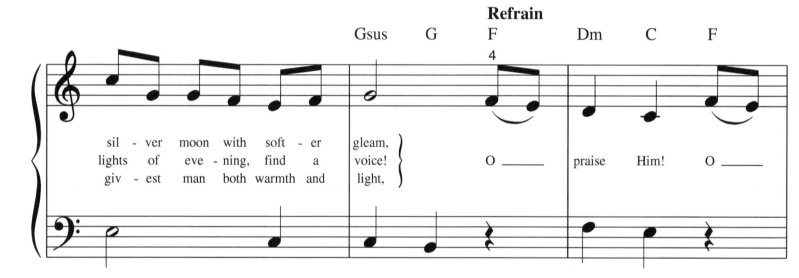

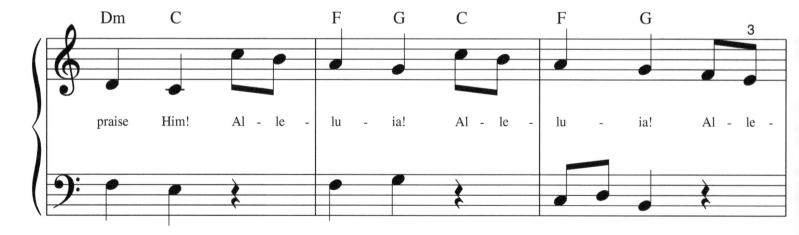

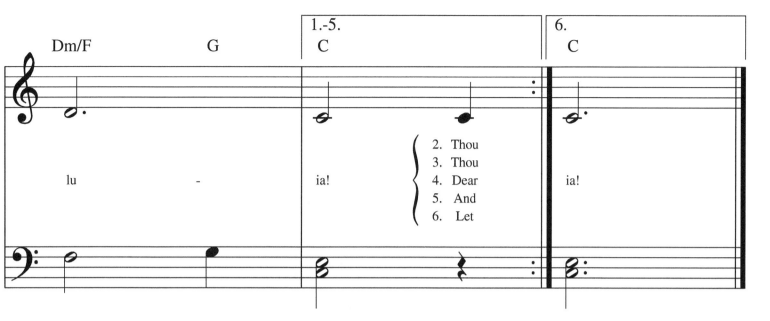

Additional Verses

4. Dear mother earth, who day by day
   Unfoldest blessings on our way,
   O praise Him! Alleluia!
   The flow'rs and fruits that in thee grow,
   Let them His glory also show!
   Refrain

5. And all ye men of tender heart,
   Forgiving others, take your part.
   O praise Him! Alleluia!
   Ye who long pain and sorrow bear,
   Praise God and on Him cast your care!
   Refrain

6. Let all things their Creator bless,
   And worship Him in humbleness.
   O praise Him! Alleluia!
   Praise, praise the Father, praise the Son,
   And praise the Spirit, Three in One!
   Refrain

BLESSED ASSURANCE

Lyrics by FANNY J. CROSBY
Music by PHOEBE PALMER KNAPP

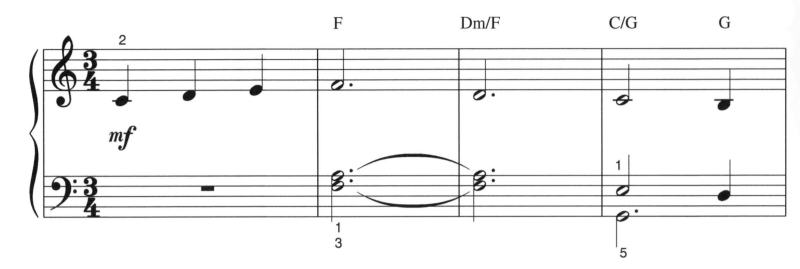

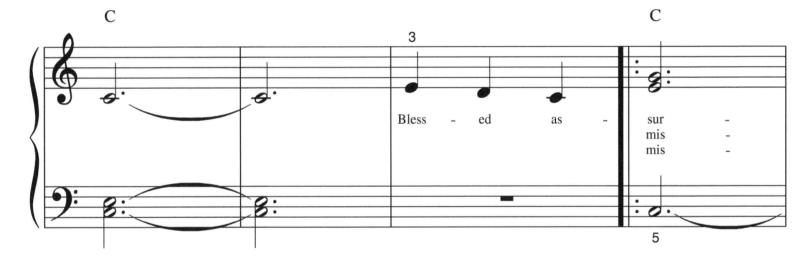

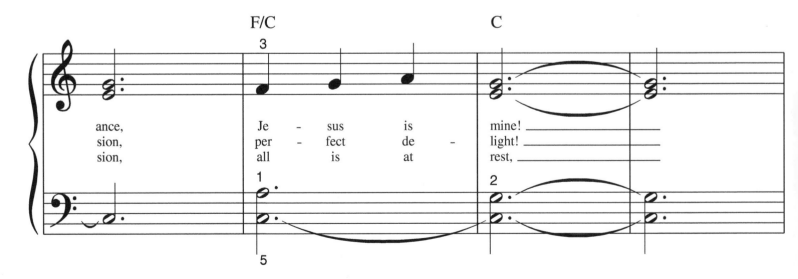

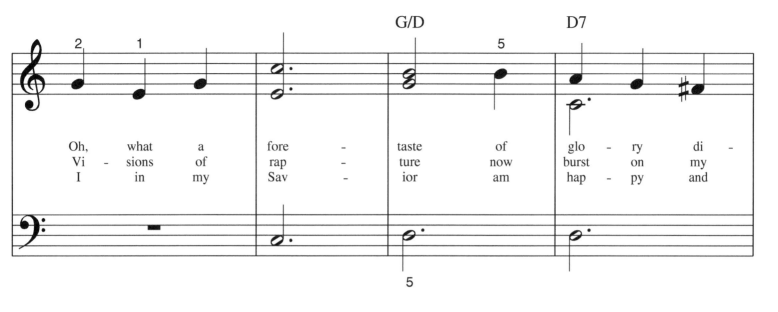

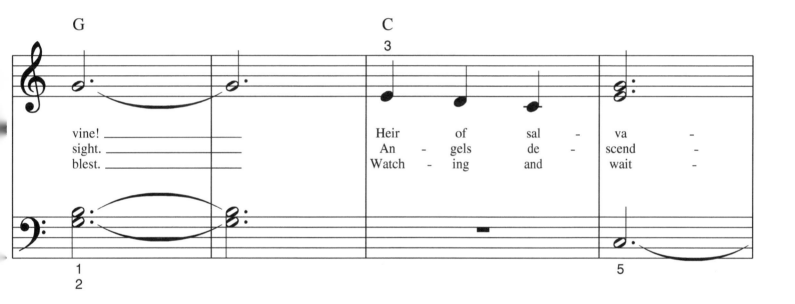

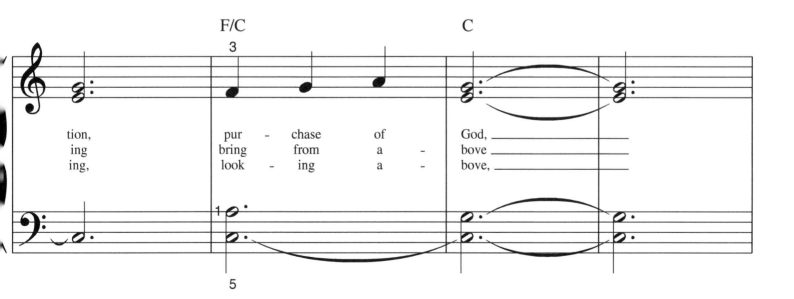

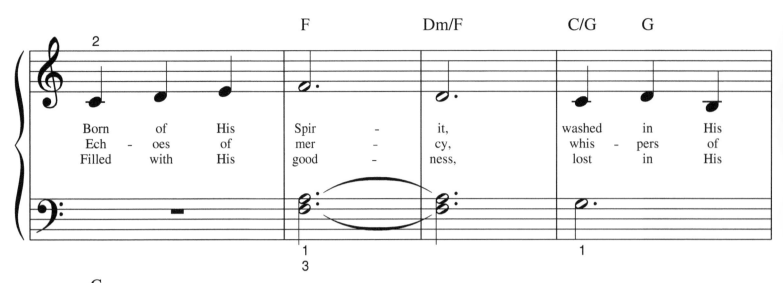

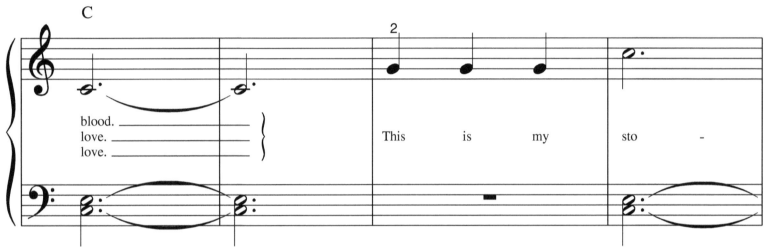

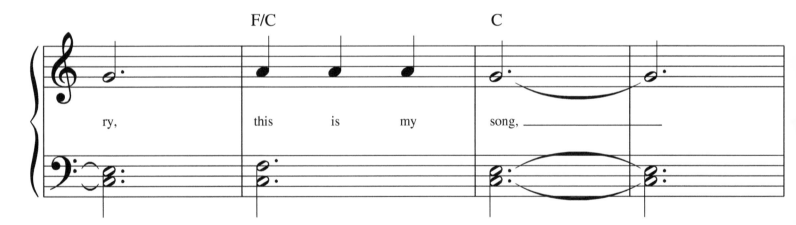

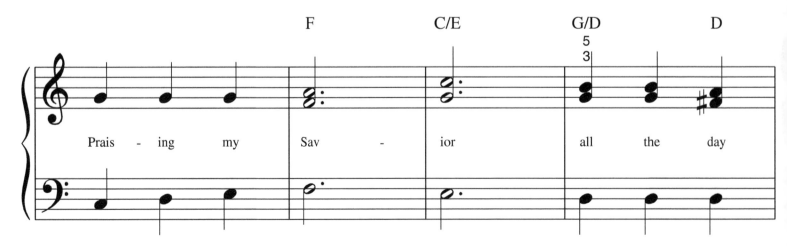

13

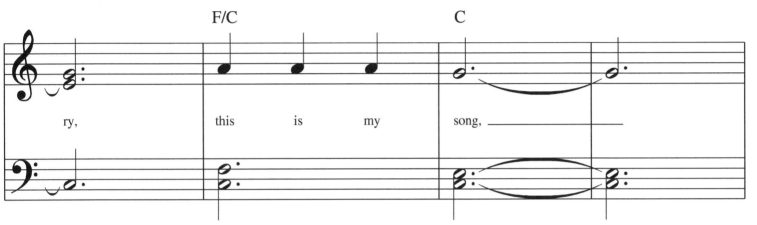

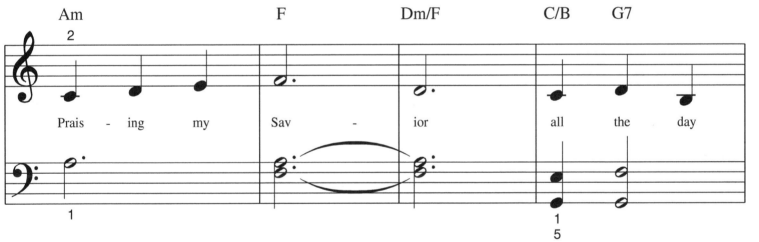

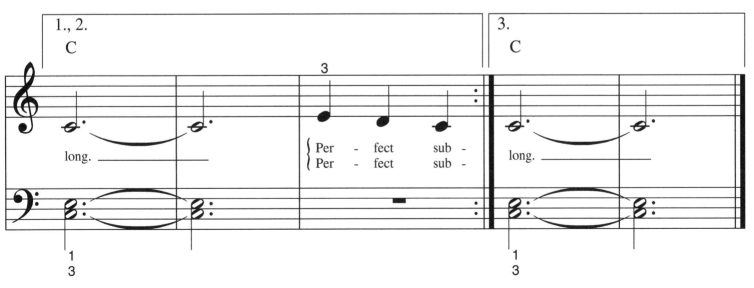

CROWN HIM WITH MANY CROWNS

Words by MATTHEW BRIDGES and GODFREY THRING
Music by GEORGE JOB ELVEY

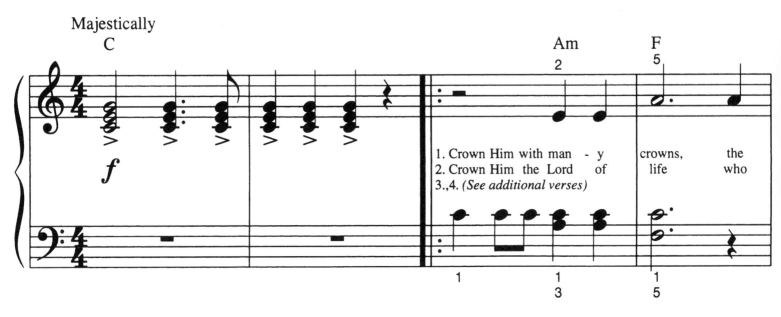

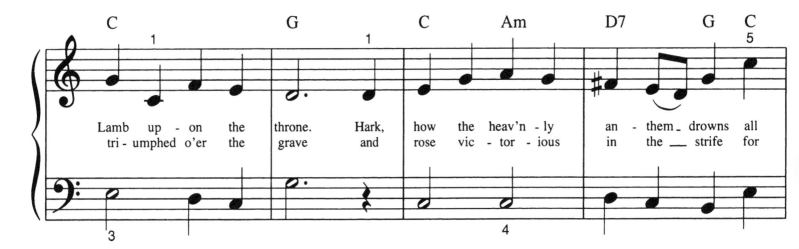

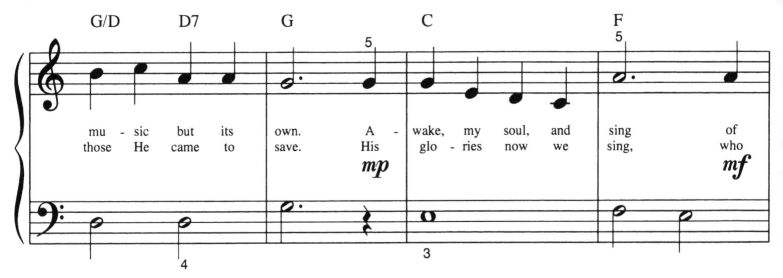

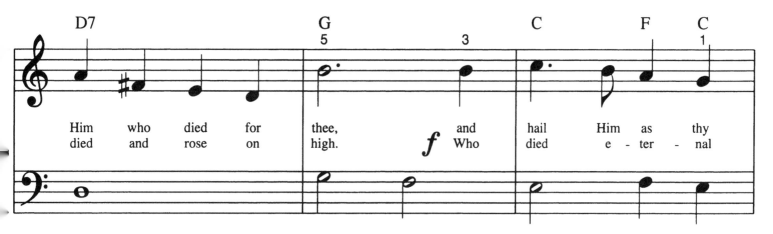

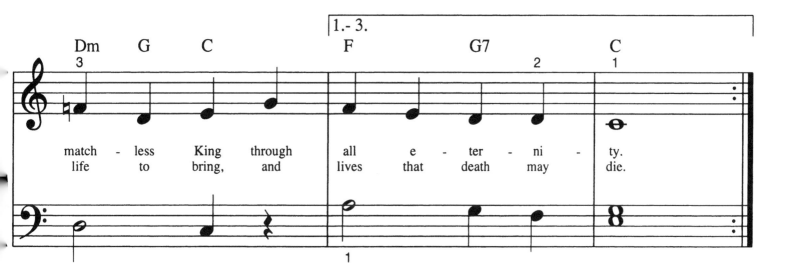

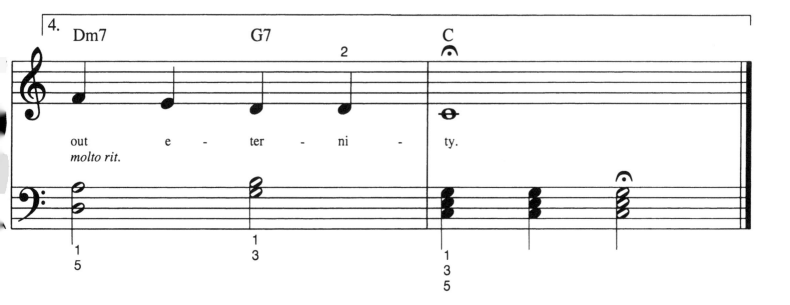

Additional Verses

3. Crown Him the Lord of peace, whose power a scepter sways
from pole to pole, that wars may cease, and all be prayer and praise.
His reign shall know no end, and round His pierced feet
fair flowers of paradise extend their fragrance ever sweet.

4. Crown Him the Lord of love; behold His hands and side,
those wounds, yet visible above, in beauty glorified.
All hail, Redeemer, hail! For Thou hast died for me;
Thy praise and glory shall not fail throughout eternity.

FOR THE BEAUTY OF THE EARTH

Words by FOLLIOT S. PIERPOINT
Music by CONRAD KOCHER

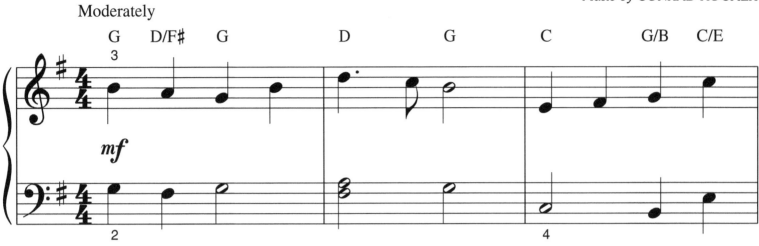

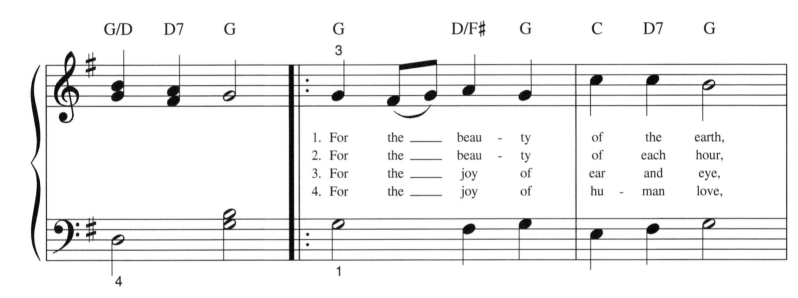

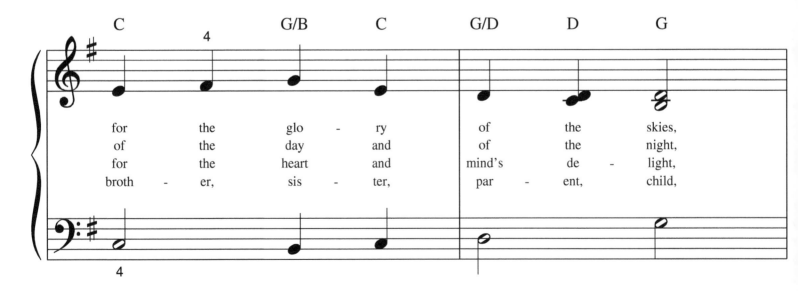

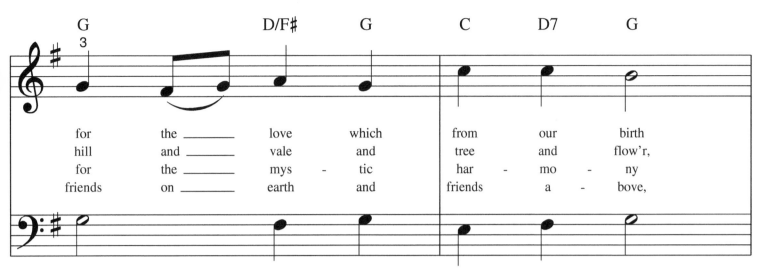

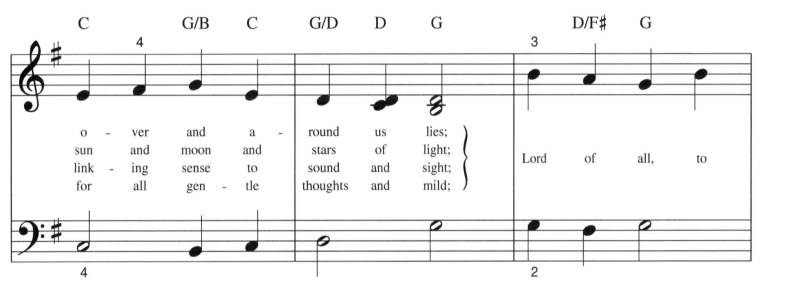

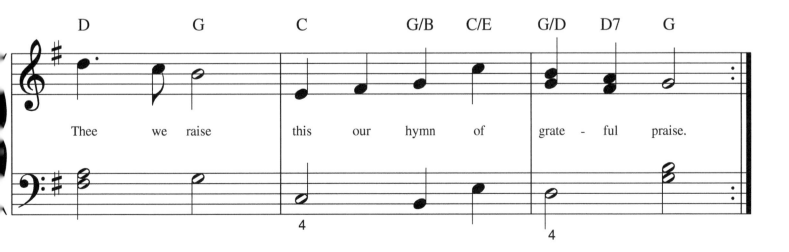

GUIDE ME, O THOU GREAT JEHOVAH

Words by WILLIAM WILLIAMS
Music by JOHN HUGHES

Stately

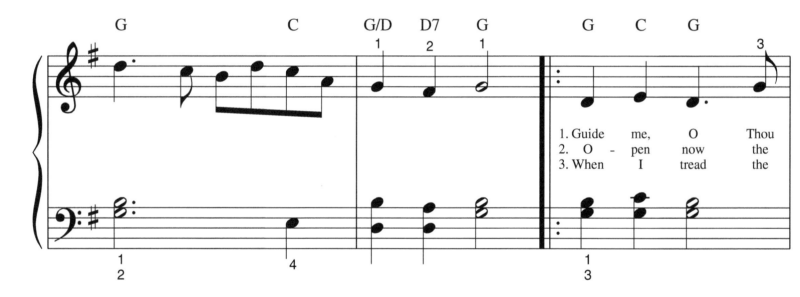

1. Guide me, O Thou
2. O - pen now the
3. When I tread the

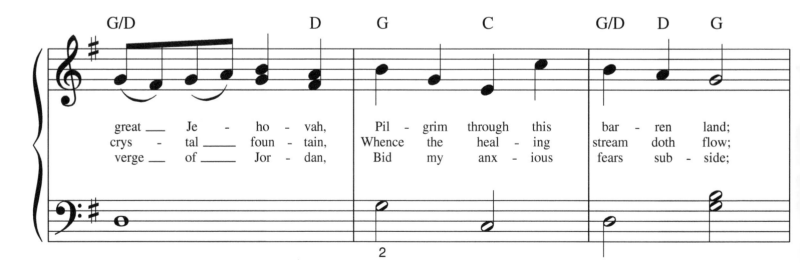

great __ Je - ho - vah, Pil - grim through this bar - ren land;
crys - tal __ foun - tain, Whence the heal - ing stream doth flow;
verge __ of __ Jor - dan, Bid my anx - ious fears sub - side;

19

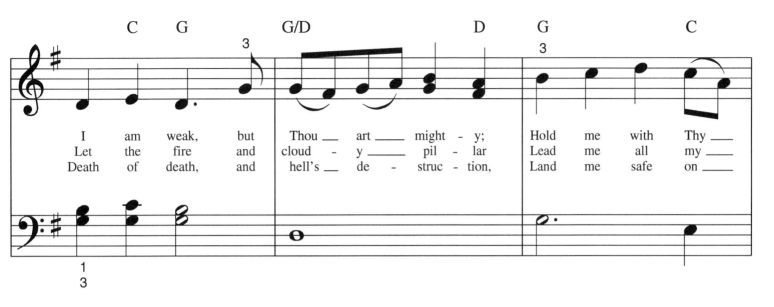

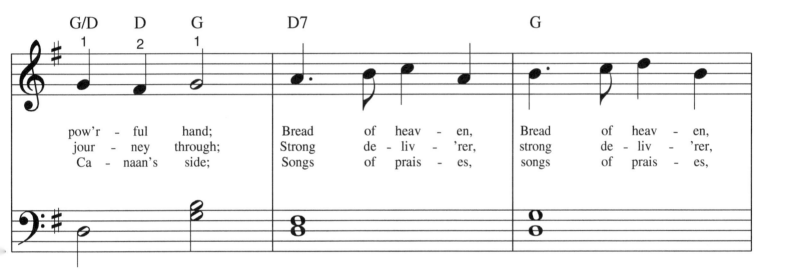

HIGHER GROUND

Words by JOHNSON OATMAN, JR.
Music by CHARLES H. GABRIEL

Moderately

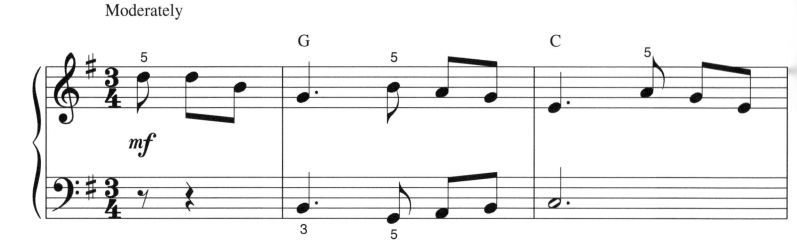

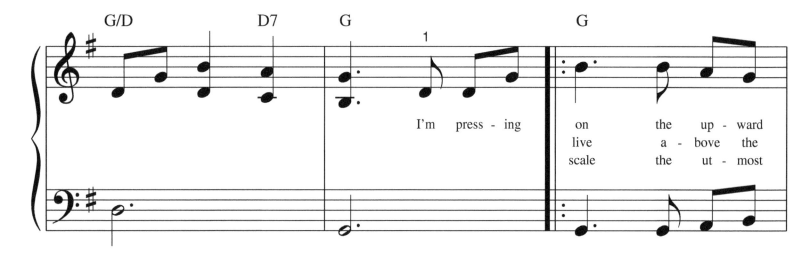

I'm press - ing on the up - ward
live a - bove the
scale the ut - most

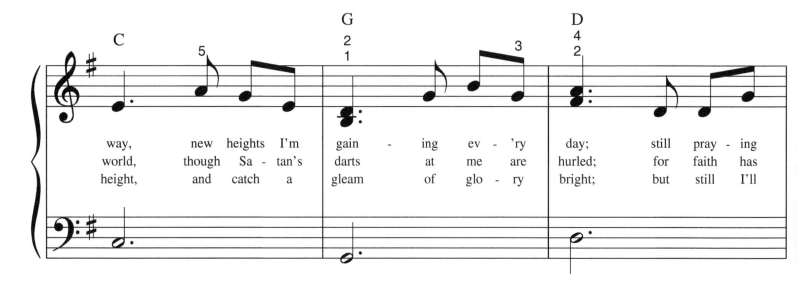

way, new heights I'm gain - ing ev - 'ry day; still pray - ing
world, though Sa - tan's darts at me are hurled; for faith has
height, and catch a gleam of glo - ry bright; but still I'll

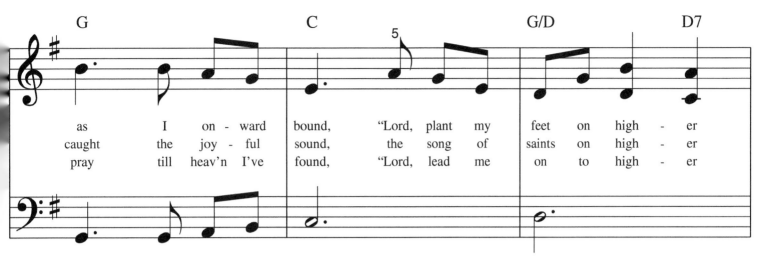

as   I   on - ward   bound,   "Lord,   plant   my   feet   on   high - er
caught   the   joy - ful   sound,   the   song   of   saints   on   high - er
pray   till   heav'n   I've   found,   "Lord,   lead   me   on   to   high - er

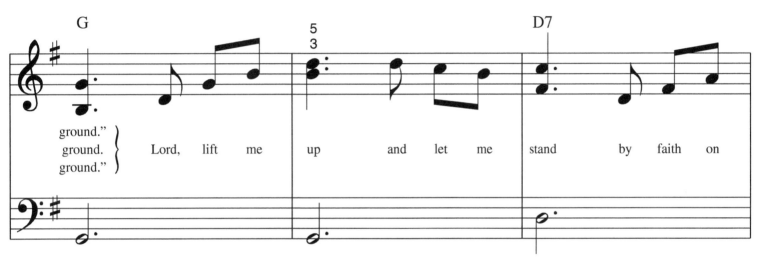

ground."
ground.}   Lord,   lift   me   up   and   let   me   stand   by   faith   on
ground."

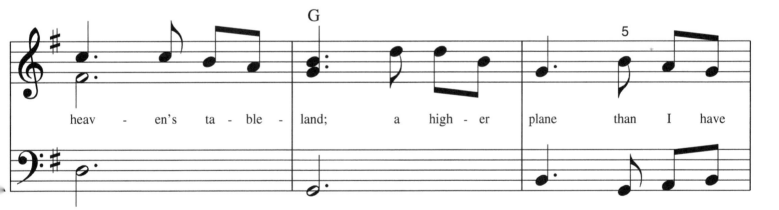

heav - en's   ta - ble -   land;   a   high - er   plane   than   I   have

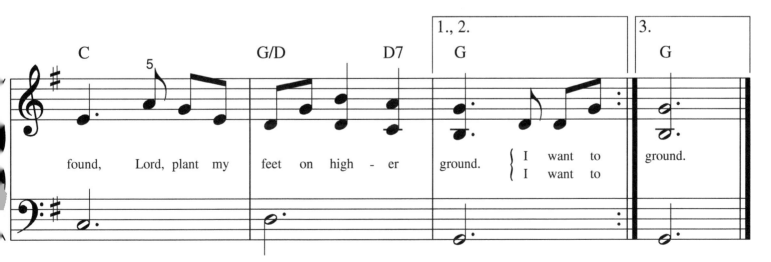

found,   Lord,   plant   my   feet   on   high - er   ground.   { I   want   to   ground.
                                                                            { I   want   to

HOLY, HOLY, HOLY

Text by REGINALD HEBER
Music by JOHN B. DYKES

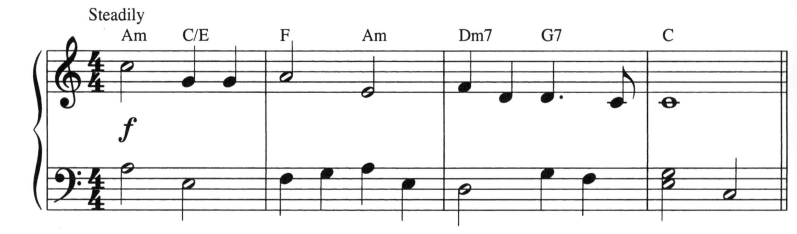

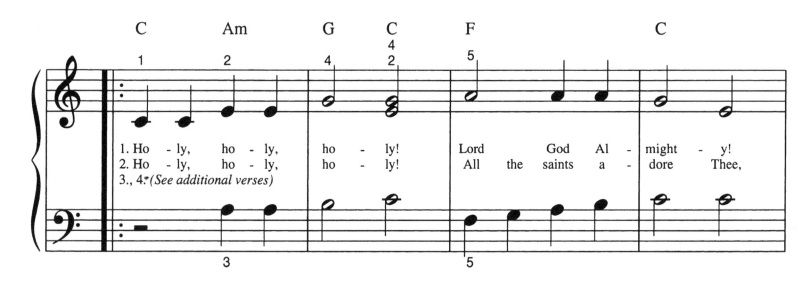

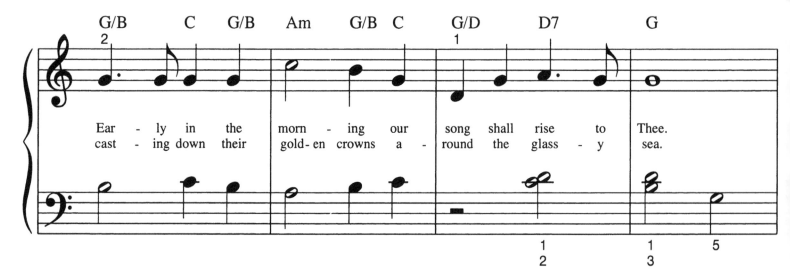

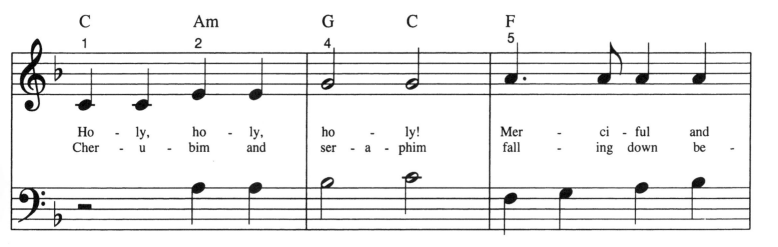

Ho - ly, ho - ly, ho - ly! Mer - ci - ful and
Cher - u - bim and ser - a - phim fall - ing down be -

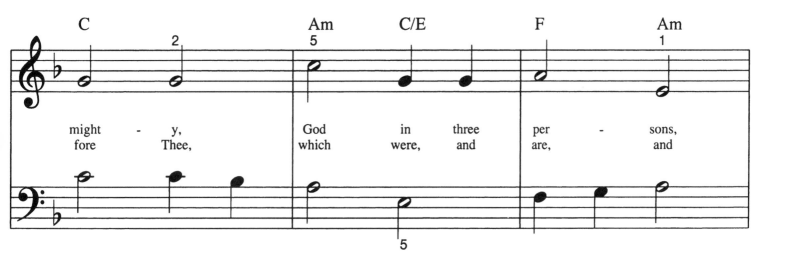

might - y, God in three per - sons,
fore Thee, which were, and are, and

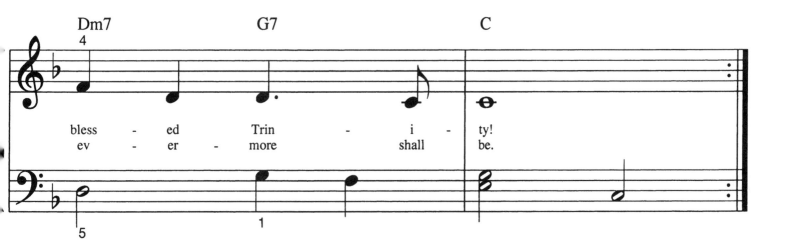

bless - ed Trin - i - ty!
ev - er - more shall be.

Additional Verses

3. Holy, holy, holy!
   Though the darkness hide Thee,
   though the eye of sinful man
   Thy glory may not see,
   only Thou art holy;
   there is none beside Thee,
   perfect in power,
   in love and purity.

4. Holy, holy, holy!
   Lord God Almighty!
   All Thy works shall praise Thy name,
   in earth and sky and sea.
   Holy, holy, holy!
   Merciful and mighty,
   God in three persons,
   blessed Trinity.

I SING THE MIGHTY POWER OF GOD

Words by ISAAC WATTS
Music from *Gesangbuch der Herzogl*

Stately

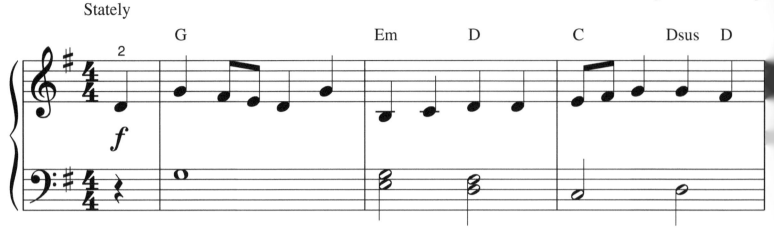

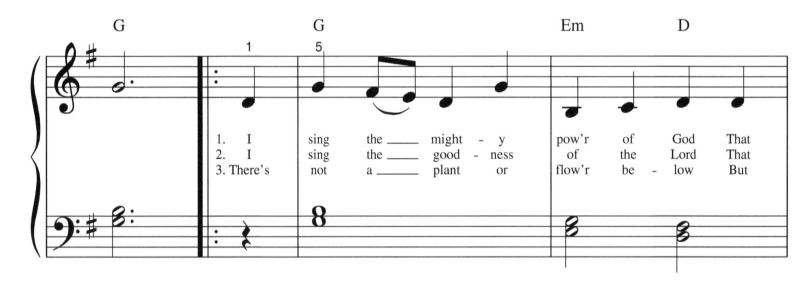

1. I sing the ___ might - y pow'r of God That
2. I sing the ___ good - ness of the Lord That
3. There's not a ___ plant or flow'r be - low But

made ___ the moun - tains rise; That spread the ___ flow - ing
filled ___ the earth with food; God formed the ___ crea - tures
makes ___ Thy glo - ries known; And clouds a - rise and

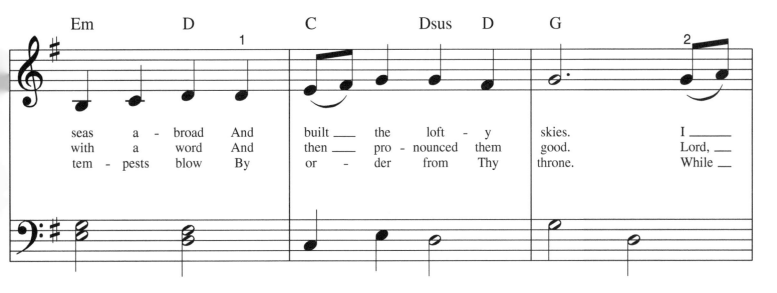

seas a - broad And built ___ the loft - y skies. I _____
with a word And then ___ pro - nounced them good. Lord, ___
tem - pests blow By or - der from Thy throne. While ___

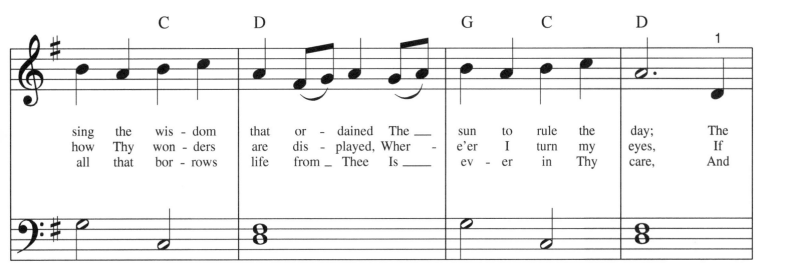

sing the wis - dom that or - dained The ___ sun to rule the day; The
how Thy won - ders are dis - played, Wher - e'er I turn my eyes, If
all that bor - rows life from _ Thee Is ___ ev - er in Thy care, And

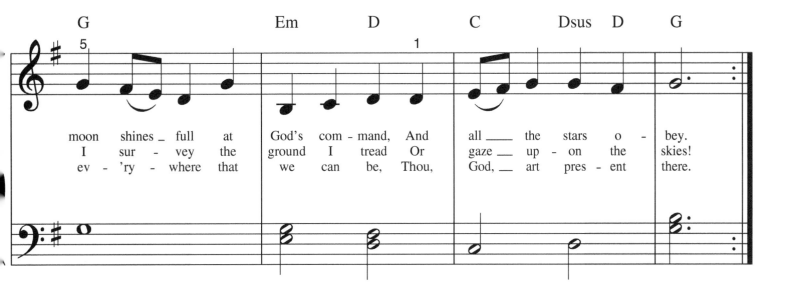

moon shines _ full at God's com - mand, And all ___ the stars o - bey.
I sur - vey the ground I tread Or gaze ___ up - on the skies!
ev - 'ry - where that we can be, Thou, God, ___ art pres - ent there.

IMMORTAL, INVISIBLE

Words by WALTER CHALMERS SMITH
Traditional Welsh Melody

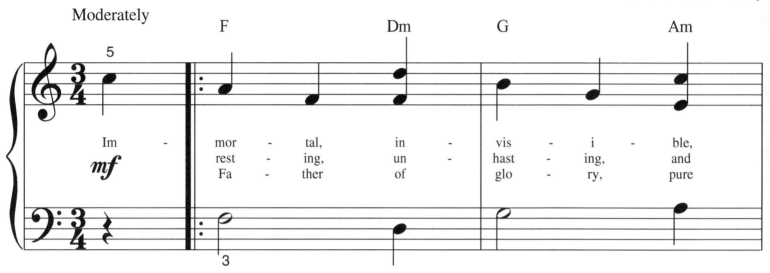

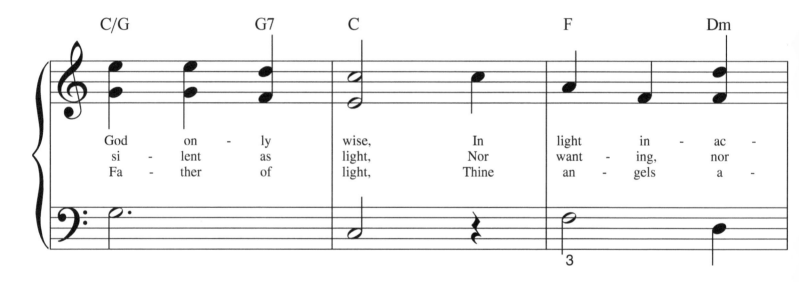

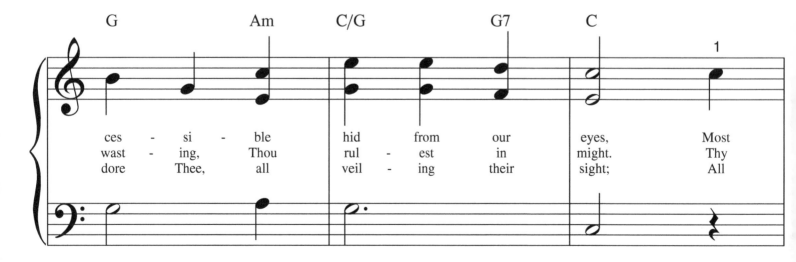

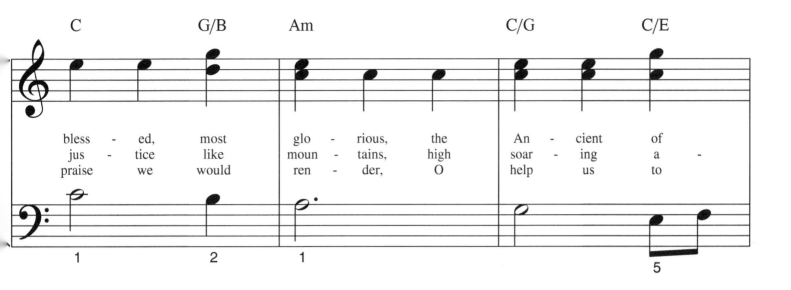

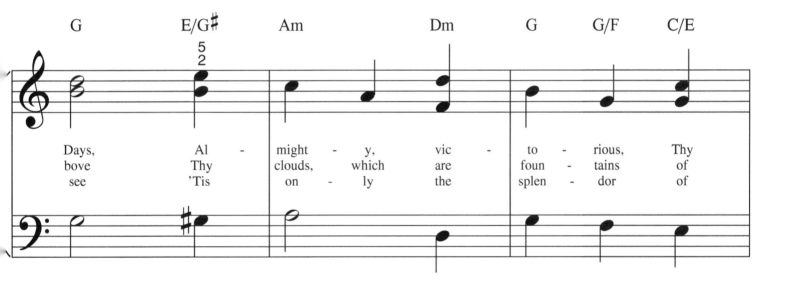

JOYFUL, JOYFUL, WE ADORE THEE

Words by HENRY VAN DYKE
Music by LUDWIG VAN BEETHOVEN,
Melody from *Ninth Symphony*
Adapted by EDWARD HODGES

Stately

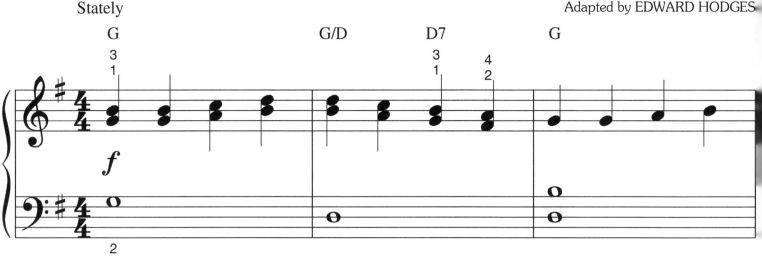

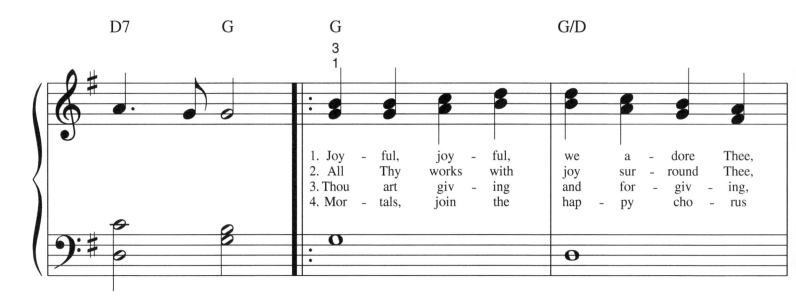

1. Joy - ful, joy - ful, we a - dore Thee,
2. All Thy works with joy sur - round Thee,
3. Thou art giv - ing and for - giv - ing,
4. Mor - tals, join the hap - py cho - rus

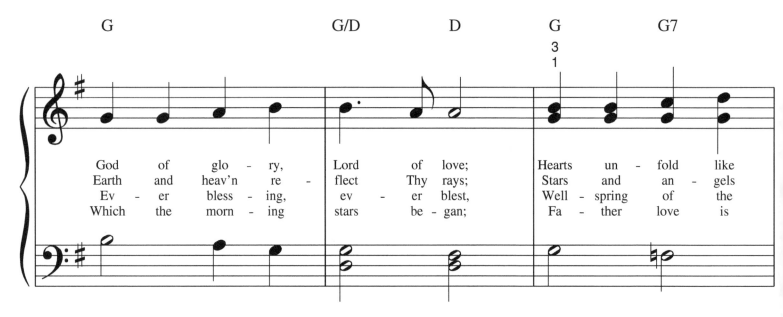

God of glo - ry, Lord of love; Hearts un - fold like
Earth and heav'n re - flect Thy rays; Stars and an - gels
Ev - er bless - ing, ev - er blest, Well - spring of the
Which the morn - ing stars be - gan; Fa - ther love is

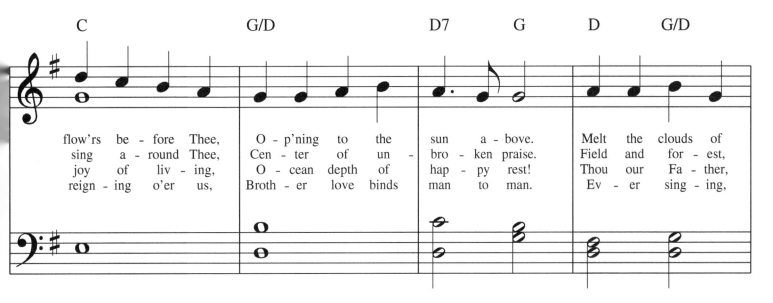

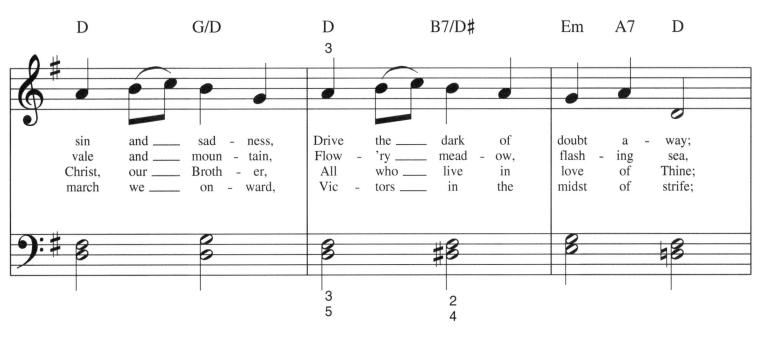

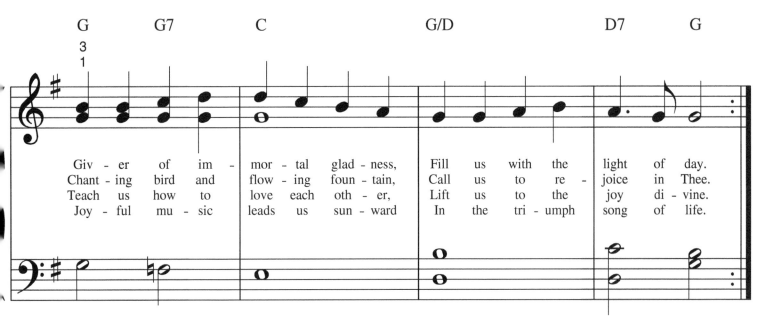

LEAD ON, O KING ETERNAL

Words by ERNEST W. SHURTLEFF
Music by HENRY T. SMART

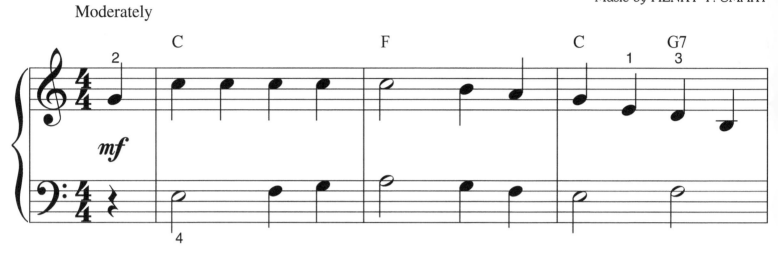

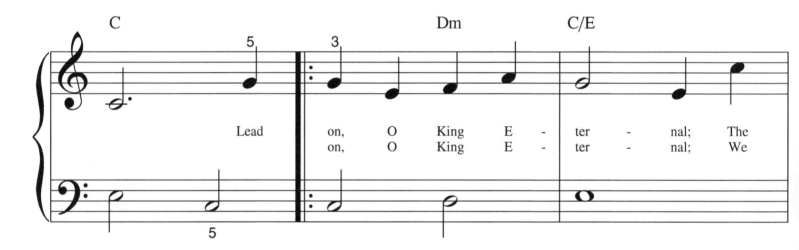

Lead
on,   O   King   E - ter - nal;   The
on,   O   King   E - ter - nal;   We

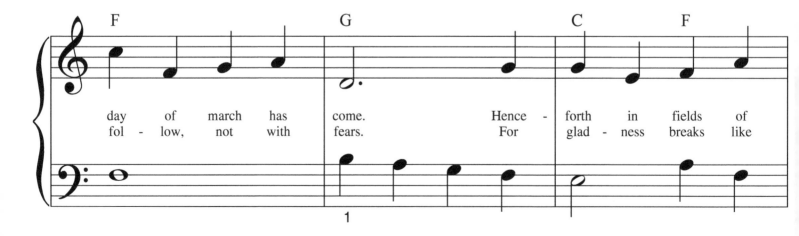

day   of   march   has   come.   Hence - forth   in   fields   of
fol - low,   not   with   fears.   For   glad - ness   breaks   like

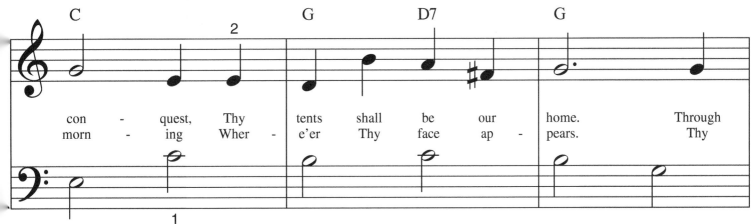

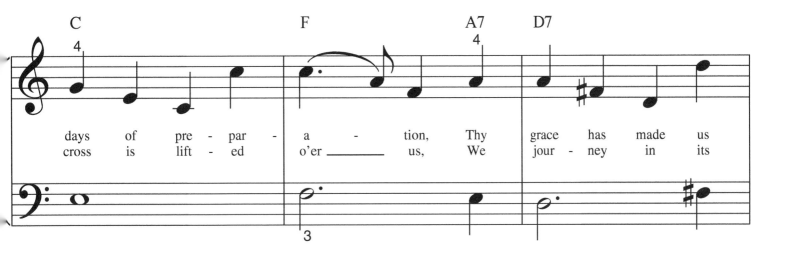

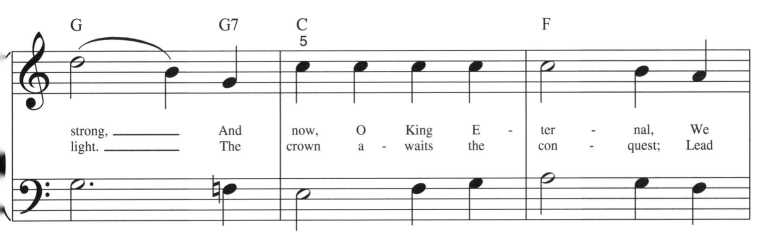

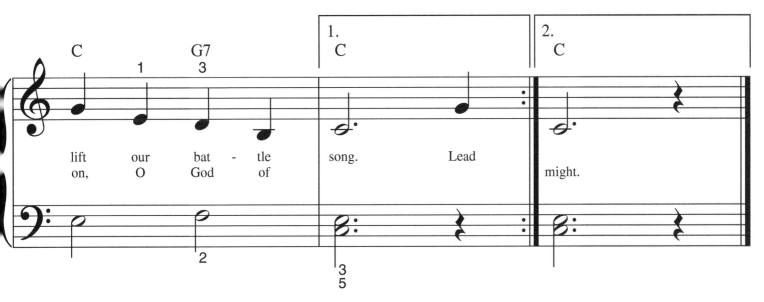

A MIGHTY FORTRESS IS OUR GOD

Words and Music by MARTIN LUTHER
Translated by FREDERICK H. HEDGE
Based on Psalm 46

Stately

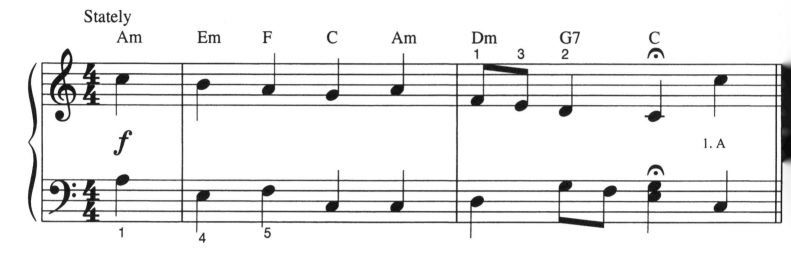

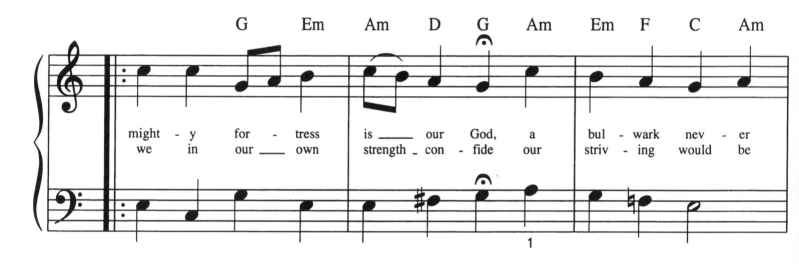

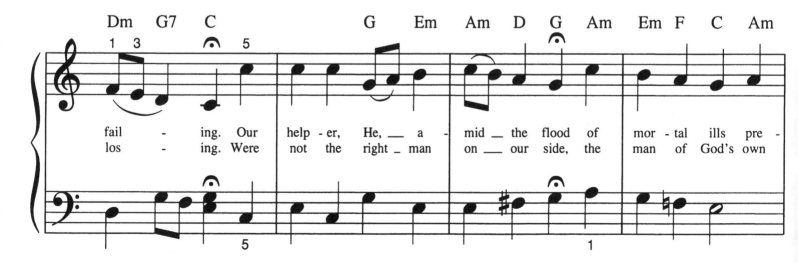

Additional Verses

3. And though this world, with devils filled,
   should threaten to undo us,
   we will not fear, for God hath willed
   His truth to triumph through us.
   The Prince of Darkness grim,
   we tremble not for him;
   his rage we can endure,
   for lo, his doom is sure;
   one little word shall fell him.

4. That word above all earthly powers,
   no thanks to them, abideth.
   The Spirit and the gifts are ours,
   through Him who with us sideth.
   Let goods and kindred go,
   this mortal life also.
   The body they may kill;
   God's truth abideth still;
   His kingdom is forever.

MY FAITH LOOKS UP TO THEE

Words by RAY PALMER
Music by LOWELL MASON

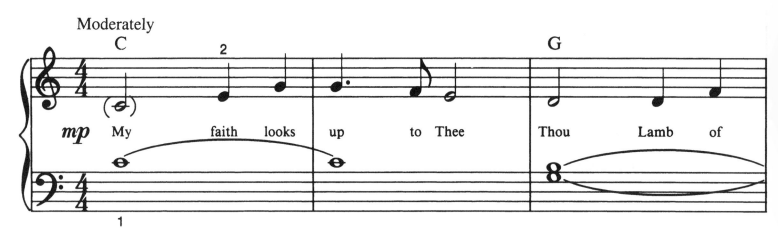

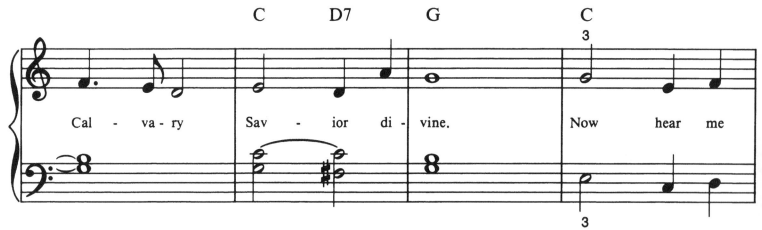

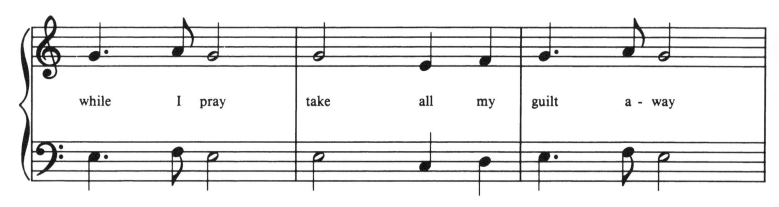

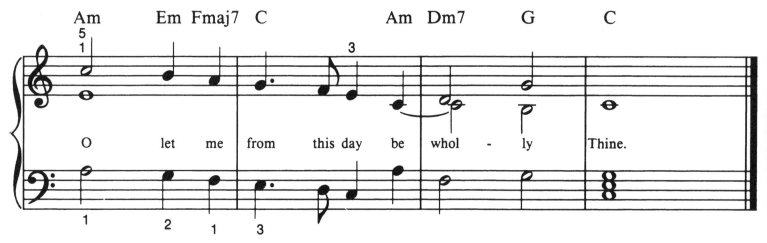

SAVIOR, LIKE A SHEPHERD LEAD US

Words from *Hymns For The Young*
Attributed to DOROTHY A. THRUPP
Music by WILLIAM B. BRADBURY

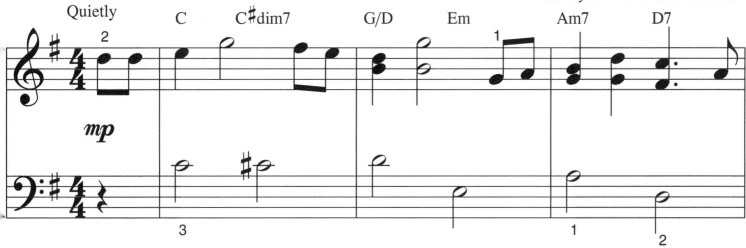

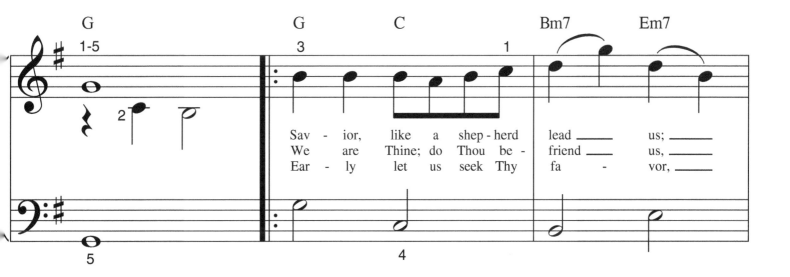

Sav - ior, like a shep - herd lead ____ us; ____
We are Thine; do Thou be - friend ____ us, ____
Ear - ly let us seek Thy fa - vor, ____

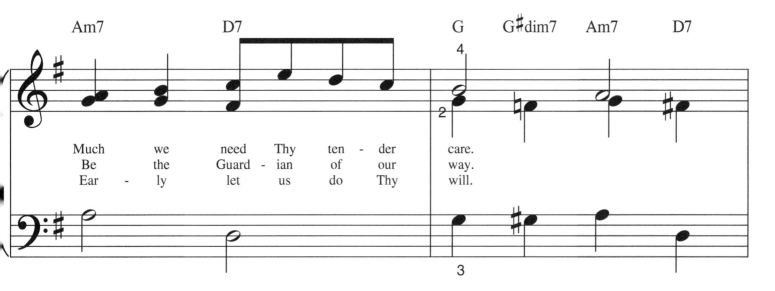

Much we need Thy ten - der care.
Be the Guard - ian of our way.
Ear - ly let us do Thy will.

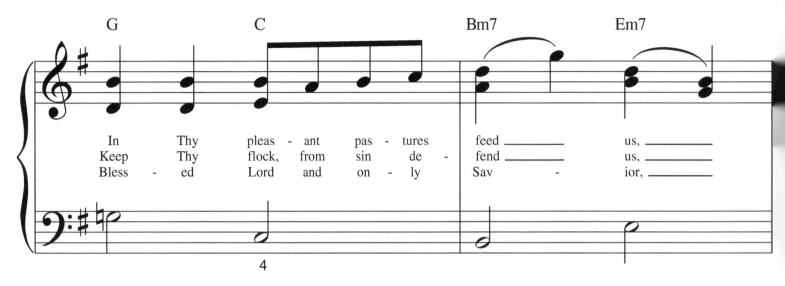

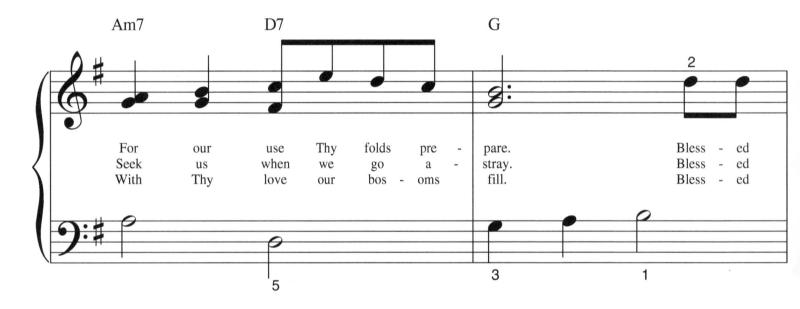

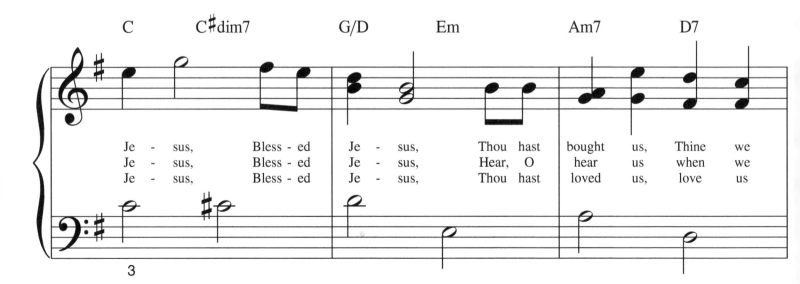

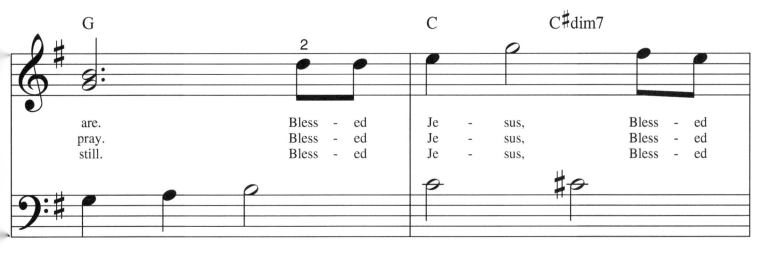

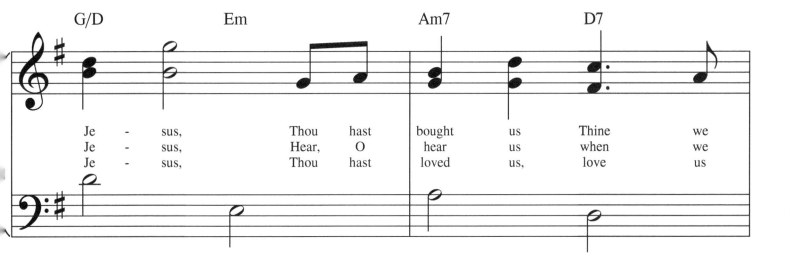

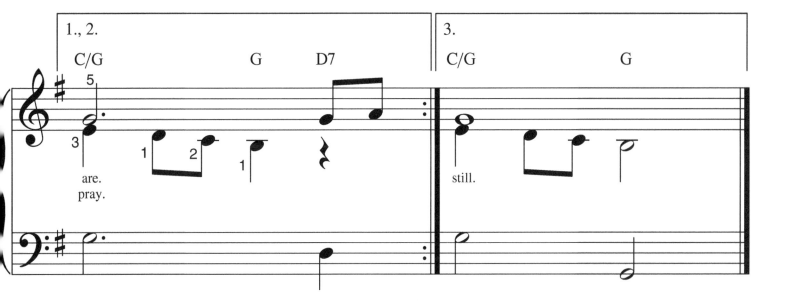

O WORSHIP THE KING

Words by ROBERT GRANT
Music attributed to JOHANN MICHAEL HAYDN
Arranged by WILLIAM GARDINER

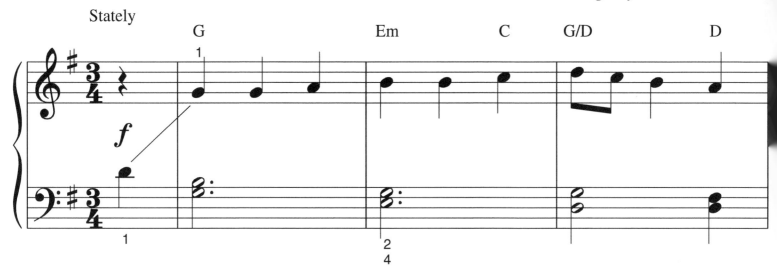

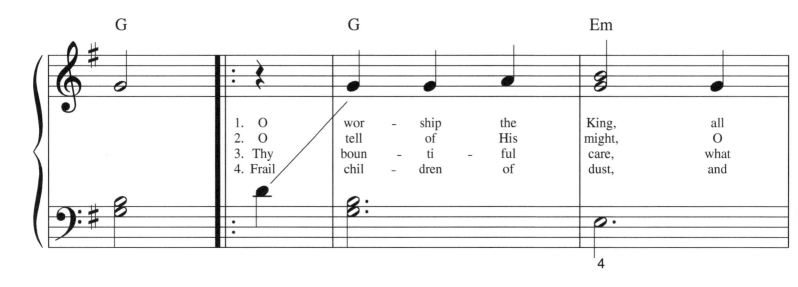

1. O wor - ship the King, all
2. O tell of His might, O
3. Thy boun - ti - ful care, O what
4. Frail chil - dren of dust, and

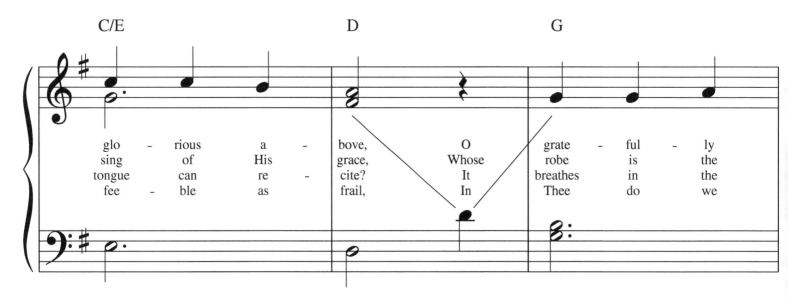

glo - rious a - bove, O grate - ful - ly
sing of His grace, Whose robe is the
tongue can re - cite? It breathes in the
fee - ble as frail, In Thee do we

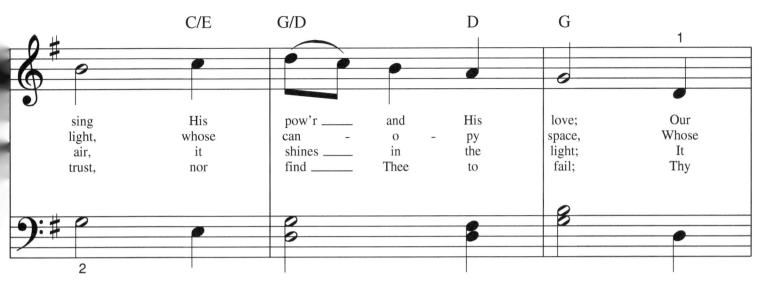

C/E   G/D   D   G

sing His pow'r ____ and His love; Our
light, whose can - o - py space, Whose
air, it shines ____ in the light; It
trust, nor find _____ Thee to fail; Thy

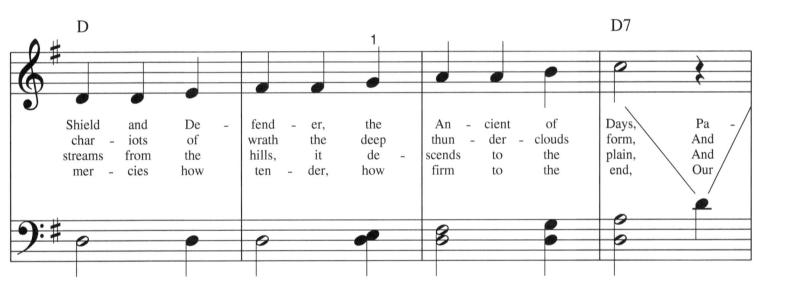

D   D7

Shield and De - fend - er, the An - cient of Days, Pa -
char - iots of wrath the deep thun - der - clouds form, And
streams from the hills, it de - scends to the plain, And
mer - cies how ten - der, how firm to the end, Our

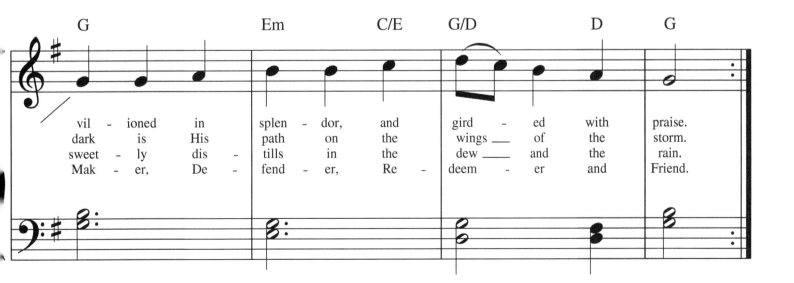

G   Em   C/E   G/D   D   G

vil - ioned in splen - dor, and gird - ed with praise.
dark is His path on the wings ____ of the storm.
sweet - ly dis - tills in the dew ____ and the rain.
Mak - er, De - fend - er, Re - deem - er and Friend.

'TIS SO SWEET TO TRUST IN JESUS

Words by LOUISA M.R. STEAD
Music by WILLIAM J. KIRKPATRICK

Flowing

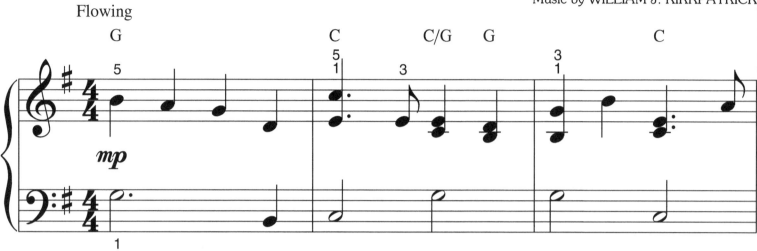

'Tis so sweet to trust in Je - sus,
O how sweet to trust in Je - sus,
I'm so glad I learned to trust Him,

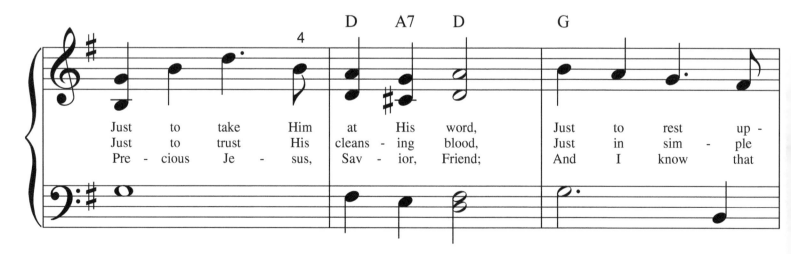

Just to take Him at His word,
Just to trust His cleans - ing blood,
Pre - cious Je - sus, Sav - ior, Friend;

Just to rest up - ple
Just in sim - ple
And I know that

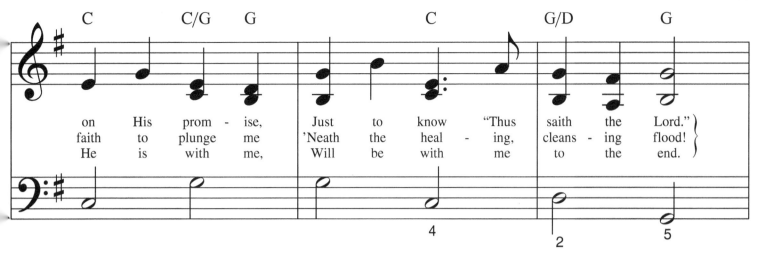

on His prom - ise, Just to know "Thus saith the Lord."
faith to plunge me 'Neath the heal - ing, cleans - ing flood!
He is with me, Will be with me to the end.

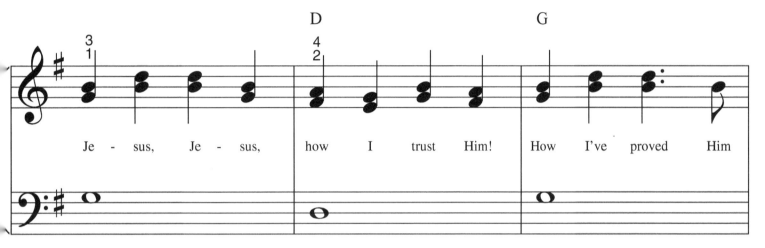

Je - sus, Je - sus, how I trust Him! How I've proved Him

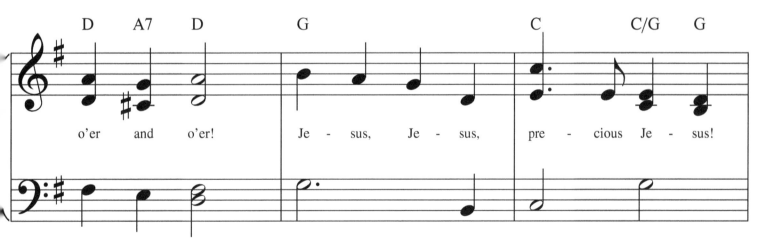

o'er and o'er! Je - sus, Je - sus, pre - cious Je - sus!

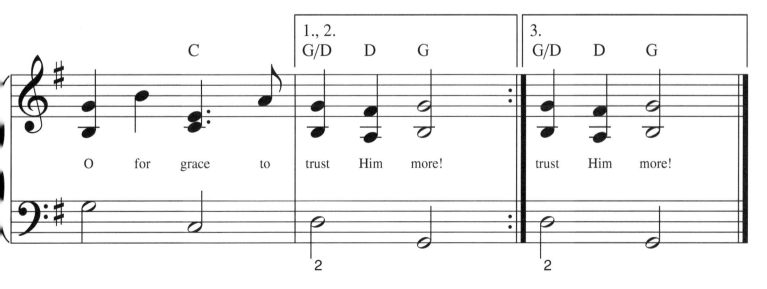

O for grace to trust Him more! trust Him more!

TO GOD BE THE GLORY

Words by FANNY J. CROSBY
Music by WILLIAM H. DOANE

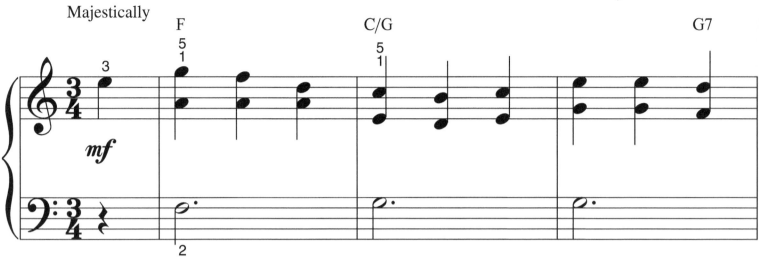

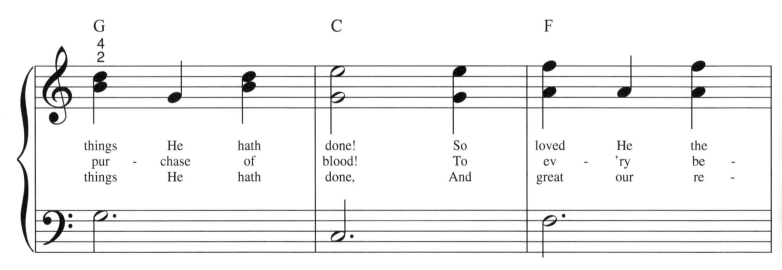

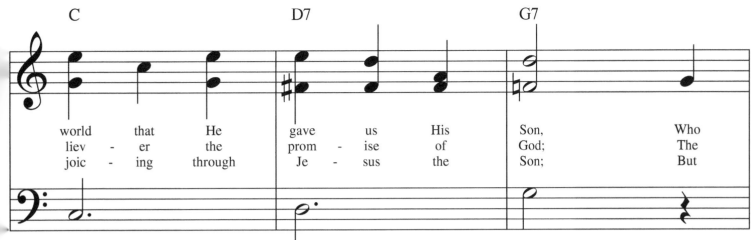

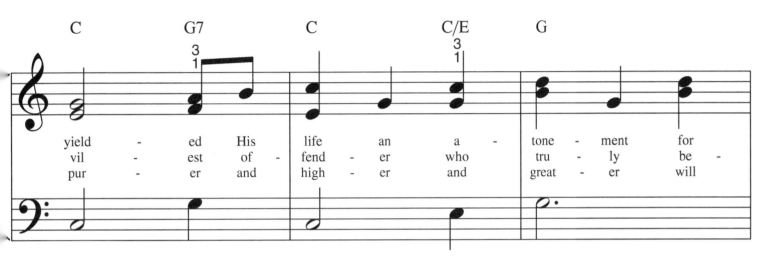

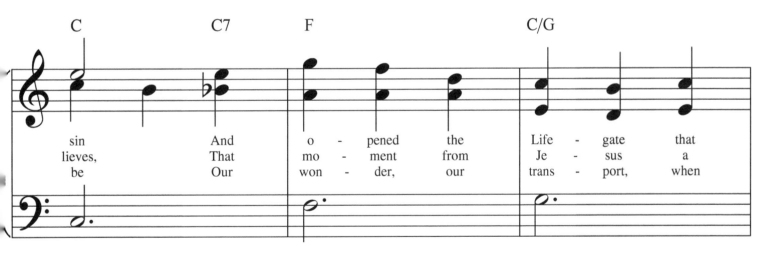

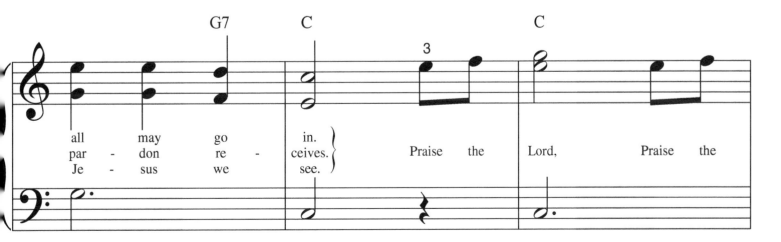

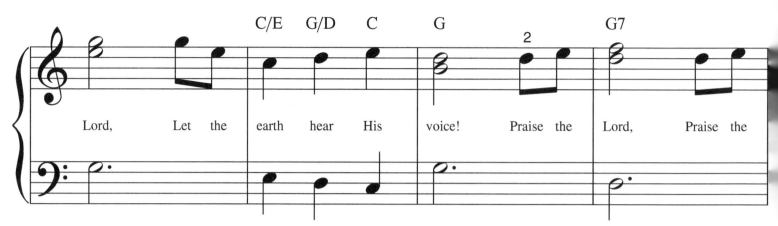

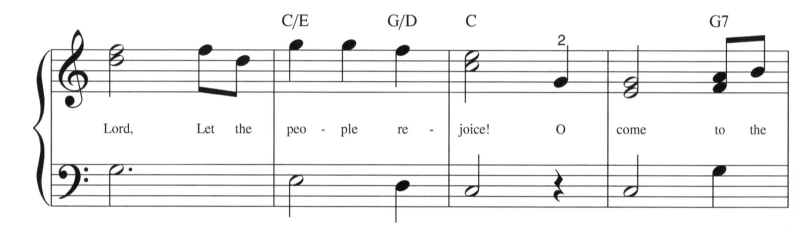

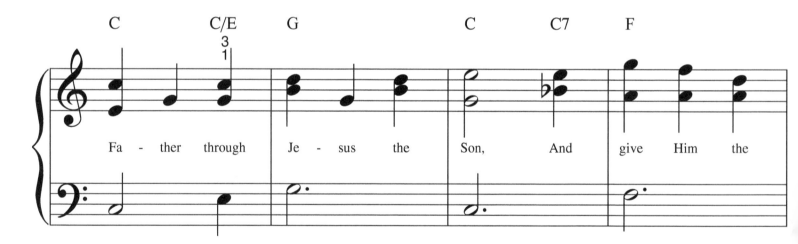

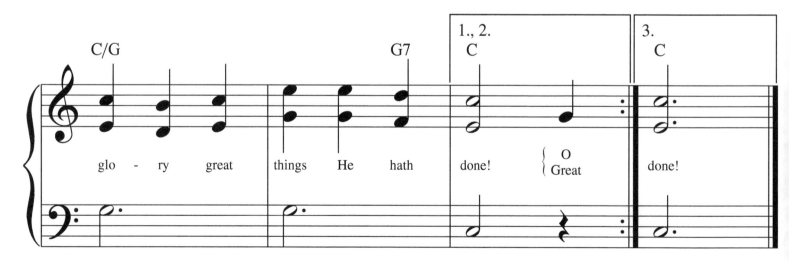

WHAT A FRIEND WE HAVE IN JESUS

Words by JOSEPH M. SCRIVEN
Music by CHARLES C. CONVERSE

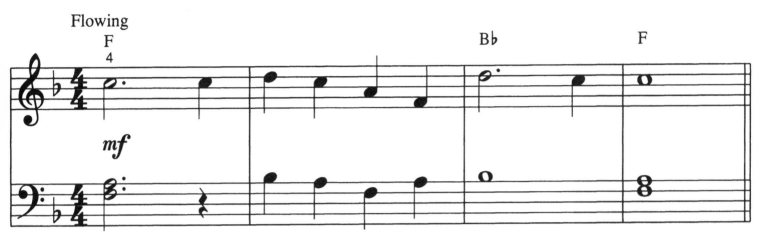

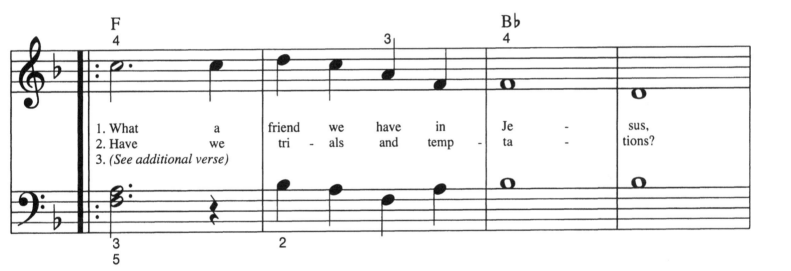

1. What a friend we have in Je - sus,
2. Have we tri - als and temp - ta - tions?
3. *(See additional verse)*

all our sins and griefs to bear!
Is there trou - ble an - y - where?

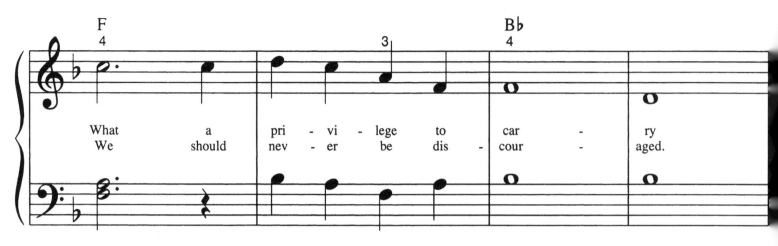

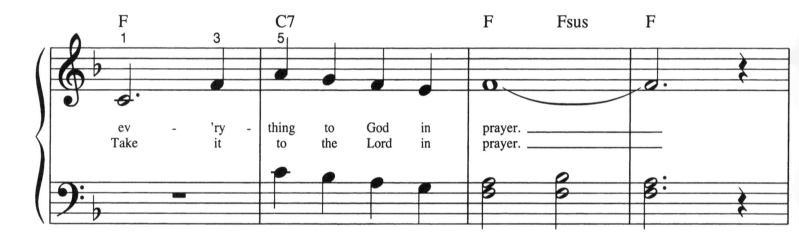

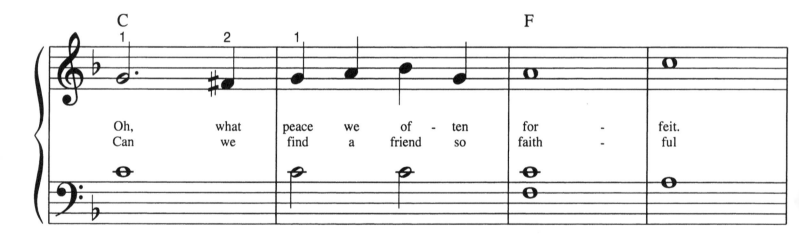

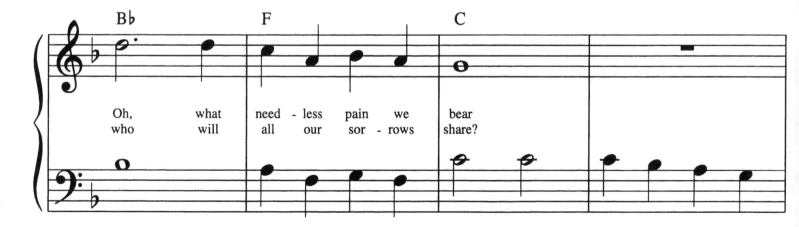

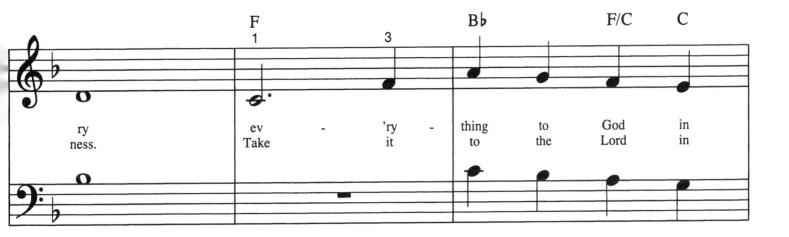

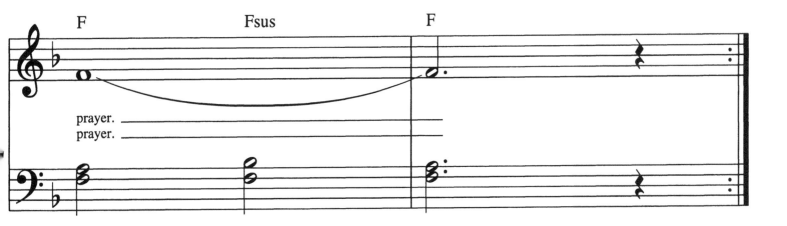

Additional Verse

3. Are we weak and heavy-laden,
   cumbered with a load of care?
   Precious Savior, still our refuge;
   take it to the Lord in prayer.
   Do thy friends despise, foresake thee?
   Take it to the Lord in prayer;
   In His arms He'll take and shield thee,
   thou wilt find a solace there.

The Best Sacred Collections for Piano

Blended Worship Piano Collection

Songs include: Amazing Grace (My Chains Are Gone) • Be Thou My Vision • I Will Rise • Joyful, Joyful, We Adore Thee • Lamb of God • Majesty • Open the Eyes of My Heart • Praise to the Lord, the Almighty • Shout to the Lord • 10,000 Reasons (Bless the Lord) • Worthy Is the Lamb • Your Name • and more.
00293528 Piano Solo...$17.99

Hymn Anthology

A beautiful collection of 60 hymns arranged for piano solo, including: Abide with Me • Be Thou My Vision • Come, Thou Fount of Every Blessing • Doxology • For the Beauty of the Earth • God of Grace and God of Glory • Holy, Holy, Holy • It Is Well with My Soul • Joyful, Joyful, We Adore Thee • Let Us Break Bread Together • A Mighty Fortress Is Our God • O God, Our Help in Ages Past • Savior, like a Shepherd Lead Us • To God Be the Glory • What a Friend We Have in Jesus • and more.
00251244 Piano Solo...$16.99

The Hymn Collection
arranged by Phillip Keveren

17 beloved hymns expertly and beautifully arranged for solo piano by Phillip Keveren. Includes: All Hail the Power of Jesus' Name • I Love to Tell the Story • I Surrender All • I've Got Peace Like a River • Were You There? • and more.
00311071 Piano Solo...$14.99

Hymn Duets
arranged by Phillip Keveren

Includes lovely duet arrangements of: All Creatures of Our God and King • I Surrender All • It Is Well with My Soul • O Sacred Head, Now Wounded • Praise to the Lord, The Almighty • Rejoice, The Lord Is King • and more.
00311544 Piano Duet...$14.99

Hymn Medleys
arranged by Phillip Keveren

Great medleys resonate with the human spirit, as do the truths in these moving hymns. Here Phillip Keveren combines 24 timeless favorites into eight lovely medleys for solo piano.
00311349 Piano Solo...$14.99

Hymns for Two
arranged by Carol Klose

12 piano duet arrangements of favorite hymns: Amazing Grace • Be Thou My Vision • Crown Him with Many Crowns • Fairest Lord Jesus • Holy, Holy, Holy • I Need Thee Every Hour • O Worship the King • What a Friend We Have in Jesus • and more.
00290544 Piano Duet...$12.99

It Is Well
10 BELOVED HYMNS FOR MEMORIAL SERVICES
arr. John Purifoy

10 peaceful, soul-stirring hymn settings appropriate for memorial services and general worship use. Titles include: Abide with Me • Amazing Grace • Be Still My Soul • For All the Saints • His Eye Is on the Sparrow • In the Garden • It Is Well with My Soul • Like a River Glorious • Rock of Ages • What a Friend We Have in Jesus.
00118920 Piano Solo...$12.99

Ragtime Gospel Classics
arr. Steven K. Tedesco

A dozen old-time gospel favorites: Because He Lives • Goodbye World Goodbye • He Touched Me • I Saw the Light • I'll Fly Away • Keep on the Firing Line • Mansion over the Hilltop • No One Ever Cared for Me like Jesus • There Will Be Peace in the Valley for Me • Victory in Jesus • What a Day That Will Be • Where Could I Go.
00142449 Piano Solo...$11.99

Ragtime Gospel Hymns
arranged by Steven Tedesco

15 traditional gospel hymns, including: At Calvary • Footsteps of Jesus • Just a Closer Walk with Thee • Leaning on the Everlasting Arms • What a Friend We Have in Jesus • When We All Get to Heaven • and more.
00311763 Piano Solo...$10.99

Sacred Classics for Solo Piano
arr. John Purifoy

10 timeless songs of faith, masterfully arranged by John Purifoy. Because He Lives • Easter Song • Glorify Thy Name • Here Am I, Send Me • I'd Rather Have Jesus • Majesty • On Eagle's Wings • There's Something About That Name • We Shall Behold Him • Worthy Is the Lamb.
00141703 Piano Solo...$14.99

Raise Your Hands
PIANO SOLOS FOR BLENDED WORSHIP
arr. Heather Sorenson

10 uplifting and worshipful solos crafted by Heather Sorenson. Come Thou Fount, Come Thou King • God of Heaven • Holy Is the Lord (with "Holy, Holy, Holy") • Holy Spirit • I Will Rise • In Christ Alone • Raise Your Hands • Revelation Song • 10,000 Reasons (Bless the Lord) • Your Name (with "All Hail the Power of Jesus' Name").
00231579 Piano Solo...$14.99

Seasonal Sunday Solos for Piano

24 blended selections grouped by occasion. Includes: Breath of Heaven (Mary's Song) • Come, Ye Thankful People, Come • Do You Hear What I Hear • God of Our Fathers • In the Name of the Lord • Mary, Did You Know? • Mighty to Save • Spirit of the Living God • The Wonderful Cross • and more.
00311971 Piano Solo...$16.99

Sunday Solos for Piano

30 blended selections, perfect for the church pianist. Songs include: All Hail the Power of Jesus' Name • Be Thou My Vision • Great Is the Lord • Here I Am to Worship • Majesty • Open the Eyes of My Heart • and many more.
00311272 Piano Solo...$17.99

More Sunday Solos for Piano

A follow-up to *Sunday Solos for Piano*, this collection features 30 more blended selections perfect for the church pianist. Includes: Agnus Dei • Come, Thou Fount of Every Blessing • The Heart of Worship • How Great Thou Art • Immortal, Invisible • O Worship the King • Shout to the Lord • Thy Word • We Fall Down • and more.
00311864 Piano Solo...$16.99

Even More Sunday Solos for Piano

30 blended selections, including: Ancient Words • Brethren, We Have Met to Worship • How Great Is Our God • Lead On, O King Eternal • Offering • Savior, Like a Shepherd Lead Us • We Bow Down • Worthy of Worship • and more.
00312098 Piano Solo...$16.99

P/V/G = Piano/Vocal/Guitar arrangements.

Prices, contents and availability subject to change without notice.

0122
001